B.A. FISHER

MONEY MAKING MACHINE

The Ultimate Guide on Money Making Methods
That Absolutely Work, Discover the Proven Ways
on How to Create Your Own Money Making Machine

Descrierea CIP a Bibliotecii Naționale a României
B.A. FISHER
   MONEY MAKING MACHINE. The Ultimate Guide on Money Making Methods That Absolutely Work, Discover the Proven Ways on How to Create Your Own Money Making Machine / B.A. Fisher – Bucharest: Editura My Ebook, 2021
   ISBN

B.A. FISHER

MONEY MAKING MACHINE
The Ultimate Guide on Money Making Methods
That Absolutely Work, Discover the Proven Ways
on How to Create Your Own Money Making Machine

My Ebook Publishing House
Bucharest, 2021

CONTENTS

INTRODUCTION	7
CHAPTER 1	9
CHAPTER 2	19
CHAPTER 3. METHOD 1	24
CHAPTER 4. METHOD 2	28
CHAPTER 5. METHOD 3	30
CHAPTER 6. METHOD 4	34
CHAPTER 7. METHOD 5	40
CONCLUSION	44

INTRODUCTION

As you (hopefully) have already discovered, making money online isn't difficult, but it does take some knowledge and the ability to put that knowledge to work.

I'm going to outline a rather simple and straight forward system that I believe anyone can use to make income. It can be scaled up as large as you like, depending on how much time you want to put into it and what you want out of it. And it's easy enough for even new marketers to do.

Mind you, this is not my invention, but rather a system that has been working for many marketers for years. It's not a shiny new bauble – instead, it's a proven method that brings home the paycheck week in and week out – if you put in the time and effort required.

Ready? Let's get started.

CHAPTER 1

1. **Choose your niche.** I'm going to make it easy for you here by recommending that you choose one of the following 3 niches: Money and finance, health and fitness, or relationships and dating. All three are evergreen and bring in a ton of money.

For purposes of this training, we're going to focus on health, because I believe it's truly the easiest of the 3 niches in which to make money.

True, there's plenty of competition, but that won't really be a factor for what we're doing. That's because people who are desperate for a health related solution such as alleviating pain or losing weight are ready to make a purchase now.

Google "most common illnesses" and you'll find acne, allergies, ADHD, arthritis, asthma, back pain, bad breath, bursitis, etc. And that's just a few from the A's and B's. $320 billion is spent on prescription drugs in the U.S. alone each year, and that doesn't include over the counter medications and remedies.

This is a HUGE market full of desperate buyers. So forget selling granny square patterns or children's bedtime stories for now – focus on where the money is.

And if you want to focus on money or relationships, those are always hot, hungry markets as well.

2. Choose a product to sell. This is going to be your OTO after they opt in to your squeeze page. Most people will tell you to create your free report, then create your squeeze page, and then find an OTO to offer after they opt in.

This is good advice. After all, they found your squeeze page, they filled out the form and they pressed the button – they are eager for a solution to their problem! Logically this is the time to offer it to them.

But I do things just a bit differently. I find the product I'm going to be promoting as my OTO first. Preferably I also find a second, similar product to use as my back up, in case the owner of the first product pulls it (yes, it happens.) The reason I find the product first is because I want to tailor my squeeze page and my free report to that EXACT topic.

For example, if my OTO is how to cure adult acne, I will write my report on ADULT acne, not teenage acne. But if I had done things the way most people do, I could have had a report on teenage acne and an OTO on adult acne. Sure it's the same problem, but it's two entirely different markets and my conversion rate on the OTO would have been terrible. That's why you want to find the product you're going to be promoting as your OTO first.

What product should you choose? Here are criteria to look for:

> *Low price* – something less than $15 is ideal because it becomes an impulse purchase. And that's exactly what you need here, because you haven't yet established a lot of credibility with your new list member.

> *Excellent product* – you've got to buy the product and make sure it really delivers on whatever it promises. This is no time to be selling junk. Actually, there is never a time to be selling junk.

> *High conversion rate* – okay, this is a no-brainer. You want a product that converts really well so that you're making money.

The ADVANCED ALTERNATIVE to promoting an affiliate product is to create your own product. The drawback is you need to create it or hire someone else to do it for you, either of which takes time. The benefit is you keep 100% of your sales, rather than splitting them with a product owner.

The CHEAT METHOD to creating your own product is of course to use some high grade PLR.

If you are using your own product, here's a trick I like to use: At the top of the sales page, let them know that their free report is on its way to their inbox. This builds consistency and credibility and shows them they're at the right place.

3. **Next you're going to create something to give away to your new niche.** Here's the key – you're not going to slap together any old report or re-purpose some PLR. Instead, you're going to create something so awesome, people would PAY YOU to get it. Best of all, you don't need to reinvent the wheel or come up with some brilliant insight to do this. Instead, you're going to let others do the research for you.

Head over to Amazon and search for your niche in the book section. Write down titles that grab your attention. Search inside the books and look at the table of contents. Take notes.

Now do the same with magazines in your niche. Look at the headlines on the magazine covers – these can be a goldmine. You'll need to change them to accommodate your exact niche (and not plagiarize) but that's easy. You want to pay attention to what the hot topics are and what headlines are used to sell those topics.

Next, visit other websites to pick up more ideas and information. This entire research process should take you about an hour or two, depending on how much time you want to put into it.

Outline the information you're going to present, and then either write your report or record it, your choice. Don't want to write it yourself? Then outsource it. It only needs to be 10 to 20 pages of solid, useful information – don't write a book.

As you go through this process, always keep in mind what you'll be promoting for your OTO, so that your freebie is 100% consistent with that product. This will give you the highest conversions on your OTO.

4. **Make your squeeze page.** Hopefully you garnered 1-5 smoking hot headlines during your research. Use these on your squeeze page as the main headline and bullets, let them know they get the report for free for opting in, and that's it. Don't make

this complicated – less is more. Create excitement and curiosity. Again, if you don't want to make your own squeeze page, you can always outsource it.

A word to the wise: Once you begin using your squeeze page, test it. Test headlines, test colors, test the call to action – just TEST. The more you test, the better conversions your page will get, the more you will make. Doesn't testing seem boring? Let me ask you this – does doubling your conversions and thus doubling what you earn seem boring? Don't think about it, just do it.

IMPORTANT: If you're using double opt in to build your list, customize the page they land on after confirming their subscription. At the top of that page, let them know their report is on its way. Then either direct them to your affiliate page if you're promoting an affiliate product, or place your sales letter on this same page. This gives them a second opportunity to purchase your offer.

5. **Get some professional articles written.** These articles have got to be outstanding, so unless you're a brilliant writer, I would suggest hiring this out to a professional.

Remember when you did your research in magazines and books? These are your very best clues as to what to write about and even how the title should read. Keep in mind: If you see something on the cover of a current magazine, that likely means it's a hot topic now and will make an excellent topic for one of your articles.

Number of articles to write: At least 2, although 30+ is better. If you're on a budget, start small and get more written later. The articles should be magazine quality. They should immediately capture attention and rivet the reader all the way to the end of the article.

Add your resource box to each article. This is your call to action where you promise the reader your shiny new report if they simply visit your totally awesome (squeeze) page.

An alternative to sending them to your squeeze page is to send them to your blog or website. Be sure to have a sign-up form on every single page of your site, offering your free report.

Variation: If you're sending your new traffic straight to your blog or website, make it for "members only." This means they have to opt in to get to your website and read the content. Yes, this is also a great way to list build. I recommend testing between the squeeze page, straight to the website with opt-in forms and making your website member's only to see which one converts the best.

6. **Find blogs in your niche.** You're looking for blogs that match your niche really well, that get lots of traffic (bare minimum - 10,000 hits a month) and that are open to guest written articles. If a blog doesn't meet all 3 of these criteria, then take a pass.

One note here: The higher traffic blogs might be harder to break in to, but they're well worth the effort. If you are more comfortable starting out with blogs of 10,000 visitors a month and working your way up, do it. After all, those 10,000 hit blogs may well be getting 100,000 visitors or more soon, and if you're already established there, so much the better.

Also, visit each blog you're considering and look at the bylines. Are all of the articles written by one author? Or does this blog accept submissions from others? While it's not impossible to get your article on a blog that is generally only written by one person, it's far easier to get it published on a blog that regularly uses guest authors.

7. **Rubber meets the road.** Remember the articles you had written?

You're going to contact these blog owners and give them your articles. Give each blog owner 2-3 articles, and only give each article away once so that each blog owner gets completely unique material from you.

Why give each blog owner 2-3 articles instead of just 1? Because you're proving that you can consistently write great articles. Also, what if the one article you send them is on a topic they don't want to cover? Or maybe they just did an article on it? By sending more than one article you give them a choice and you also greatly increase the odds that they will publish at least one article for you.

Here's how you give the articles away: Contact these people. Do it through email, through Facebook, through Skype, whatever. Better yet, contact them through all of those methods at the same time. No, you're not spamming them. You are HELPING them. Send them a very friendly, upbeat message that includes the following points:

- You've been reading their blog
- You love what they write
- You've written exclusive articles just for them
- The articles are free – they can do whatever they want with them

- No strings attached

- You would like (LOVE!) to be a guest writer on their blog

- If they would publish one of your articles on their blog with your author's box to help you get exposure, that would be totally awesome

- Thank you

CHAPTER 2

What you've just done:

❑ You've made contact and you've GIVEN them something right off the bat, no strings attached. What happens when 99 out of 100 people contact a blog owner? They WANT something. But you are GIVING something, and it's something totally cool, too: Well written articles that are perfect their blog.

❑ You've got a new contact in your field. Do you think s/he might want more articles? And maybe they will even promote one of your own products? It could happen, and it starts with this initial contact.

❑ You've solved a problem for this new contact – you've given him or her high quality content. If you're a blog owner, you know how hard it can be to create new content week after week. Having help is always much appreciated.

❏ You've got some serious link juice going. You're contacting BIG blogs with major traffic, many of which will be posting your articles. Think Google will notice? Absolutely!

❏ You've got traffic. FREE traffic. Highly TARGETED, raving fanatical traffic visiting your website.

❏ You are building a LIST out of this traffic. A list of highly targeted people who think you must be an expert because you write articles on important blogs. Traffic that reads your stuff. Traffic that BUYS your stuff.

❏ You are making money immediately with your OTO. Remember, you've got a low priced and highly targeted OTO after your squeeze page.

This product is something directly related to the issue you wrote about in the article and in the report.

Total cost for this list building/product selling business? If you do everything yourself, it costs you nothing but time. If you outsource the squeeze page and articles, it might run you a couple of hundred dollars, more or less.

What do you do now? Rinse and repeat. Continue writing articles (or having someone write articles for you) and continue contacting new blogs. Write more articles for the blogs on which you've already been published.

This works. Don't reinvent the wheel – just do it.

The downside is you will find a few blog owners who simply won't publish your stuff. That's okay. Most times they will tell you that they won't, and then you can take those same articles and offer them to a different blog.

Killer Tip: A variation to sending them 2-3 articles is to send one 3-part series. It's got to be totally researched, relevant and on a hot topic. If you get them to publish this (generally over the course of 3-5 days) you will see even more traffic than you would from getting one regular article published.

Now let's talk hypothetical numbers just to get a feel for what this system can do for you: You contact one blog that gets 250,000 visitors a month. 25% of them read your article (that's kind of a low number – you might get more.) Of those who read your article, 40% click your link, and 50% of those get your free report (meaning they joined your list.)

That's 250,000 times .25, which is 62,500 people who read your article. How cool is that?? Just imagine for a second that 62,500 people read your article and see your byline – you're already an expert and they haven't even clicked on your author's resource box yet.

Of those 62,500 people, 40% click your link. That's 25,000 people going to your squeeze page. I don't know about you, but when I think about getting 25,000 HIGHLY targeted people to my squeeze page, my heart beats a little faster and you can't wipe the grin off my face.

Of those, we're hypothetically saying that half join your list. I know some of you are thinking that number is high, and for the typical squeeze page it is high. But in this case they've just read your article on a high authority website and obviously liked it. They already know why they are coming to your page (to get your super-duper hot report on a topic they're really interested in) and so you unless your squeeze page totally sucks, you can expect to get a higher than average conversion.

Half of 25,000 is 12,500 new people on your list. People who have read your article. People who think you're pretty hot stuff. People who are now going to read your report and KNOW you are pretty hot stuff. People who are far more likely than average to open and read your emails.

12,500 people from one article. Okay, true, you had several articles written and probably sent 3 of those to the blog owner, who maybe only published one. Still – is that a good return on your time and money or what???

And if you only do $1/10^{th}$ as well as our example? Then you still have 1,250 highly targeted new subscribers. Not bad.

To those skeptics who think that only the "big dogs" can make money online, I hope I have just given you something to think about, and more importantly a plan of ACTION.

One more number I want to throw out here: Suppose you got 12,500 new subscribers per month. Maybe you did it with one article, maybe it took you 20 articles. Whatever. Each month you do what it takes to get 12,500 how new subscribers. Assuming a high attrition rate of 20%, how many subscribers would you have by the next holiday season?

I'll leave you to do your own math on this one.

CHAPTER 3

METHOD 1

You've seen the steps that can make you money today. This portion would discuss those that are more left field out of the box kind of money making.

Now these methods are not similar in nature but they all have one thing incommon, they make money and they can make it fast!

My advice is to outsource all of these methods. Learn them, understand them andapply them then outsource them so you are not doing all the work yourself.

Like I said this isn't traditional Internet Marketing stuff this is all about makingmoney online by any means possible.

This is a relatively simple method but it can bring in a lot of cash for you very quickly. I highly recommend you outsource all the work here simply because the demand you will receive will be too much for just one person to handle.

This isn't necessary a new method but the fact is that it works. Ok this somewhat involves offline marketing because basically what you do is pace a newspaper ad in your local newspaper advertising that you will set up a website for free. This attracts a lot of local businesses who want to get a website up and running.

It's best if you provide some templates and give them the option of what they like best and tell them to provide you with all the content including logos and picturesetc.

Now for the money part. They are going to need some webhosting so you simply get them to sign up for an account using your affiliate link. Now most people won't have a problem signing up through your affiliate link because you have already provided them with a free website. A lot of the time people won't even notice because they are offline business people and some are not even aware ofwhat an affiliate program is.

If you want you can use a domain redirect to change your affiliate URL but in all honesty I don't think it is really a problem.

Now there are lots of different webhosting companies that you can choose from but I prefer to stick with the big names.

They are familiar, they have a proven record of paying out their affiliates and they offer an easy professional service.

I think HostGator offer a really good service. It's quick and easy to sign up as an affiliate and they provide a professional service so your client will be happy. They also offer live online support which is an added bonus. Their payment plans increase with the number of new customers you bring in as you can see below. If you are bringing in really big numbers you will be able to negotiate with them to increase your commissions.

As you can see from the screenshot above you just need 21 sign-ups to make $2,625 a month. You will get a LOT MORE response from posting an ad in the newspaper and you will easily make over 21 sign-ups in your first month. But as you can see you really need to outsource this kind of stuff.

Doing 21 websites by yourself even though they are just simple templates with the content already provided can be time consuming. But if you have a team set up that will get the website up and running as soon as an order comes in you will be able to process 100's of orders every month and make a very handsome profit.

When placing your newspaper ad I prefer to set up a new email account at gmail.com to handle all the inquiries. You can put your phone number in the ad if you want to but personally I don't like getting calls all day so I just set up a new email account and in the ad I tell people to send an email inquiry. It's simple and easy that way and I just correspond with them through email.

This is a simple but very powerful method. The best part is since it's all done over the Internet you can advertise in any newspaper you want. If you set up an entire outsourcing team to handle this operation you can advertise in a big city mainstream newspaper and bring in 1000's of new customers in one hit.

This is a very profitable opportunity and one that can be set up quickly and easily. Below you will find the resources you need to set this up.

CHAPTER 4

METHOD 2

Ok this method involves getting paid for creating articles. This is a REALLY simple method but if you put it to use you will make money. Again this can be scaled up if you outsource this.

Basically the method goes like this: you create as many articles as you can and you submit them to websites who pay you for new content and you collect the rewards.

Now in theory this sounds good but obviously you are going to need to have a whole heap of fresh new articles coming in all the time for this to be worthwhile. You could manually sit and write them but if you are anything like me that is the last thing you want to do.

So we have a couple of alternatives. Firstly you can obviously outsource your articles. But make sure that you are getting quality unique content not PLR articles that are shared between lots of people.

Or you can use a piece of software that makes the process a whole lot easier. It's a voice recognition software called "Dragon Naturally Speaking" which enables you to speak your articles while the program writes them.

This is a massive time saver and you are able to produce a lot of articles using this method. It's just like someone dictating you.

The best way to do this is chose a topic that you are actually interested in that way you will be able to speak your mind without needing any reference.

Simply fire up the program and start talking, don't worry about mistakes or grammatical errors at this point you can correct them later. Your main focus is to get as many articles done as possible.

CHAPTER 5

METHOD 3

Ok this is a really quick and easy method that doesn't require much work at all butI thought I would include it because it's super quick and easy and it can bring in a nice passive income. This method works best in volume, so this is something you should get outsourced for sure.

This method involves taking advantage of people misspelling domain names. What we do is register all the common misspellings of popular sites and set up a domain redirect for our affiliate program.

If you don't know how to do a domain redirect it is very easy. You have to have your own website and hosting obviously and depending on what company you are with there will be an icon in your control panel. It will look something like theimage below.

Then you simple enter your affiliate URL and your domain will get redirected to your affiliate page. Easy!

Porn sites seem to convert best for this method because people who are searching for porn aren't really that fussed about which site they are on as long as there is porn.

So the best way to do this is join as many porn affiliate programs as possible and then try and find their misspellings. Some examples of misspellings are: "reddtube.com" "youponr.com" "googl.com" etc.

The best ones are simple mistakes like having the "ie" or "ou" switched around the wrong way or the last two letters switched. Another good one is the key on the keyboard that is either side to the letter.

You can do this in other areas besides porn but porn converts best because it's a broad topic and people are not as partial to the particular site as long as it provides what they are looking for. Whereas people trying to get to ebay might not want to sell their item on another site so they will go back to ebay.

Dating sites also work well and you can find misspellings for a lot of them.

Ok so what you want to do is first create a list of sites you want to target. Do this by checking out the Alexa top 500 list here: http://www.alexa.com/site/ds/top_500

Then start joining affiliate programs related to that niche. If you chose to promote porn then simple do a google search for "adult affiliate programs" and you will find a healthy list to choose from.

Next you want to find all the misspellings for that domain. This can be a little time consuming so I recommend you outsource this project to save time. However if you want to have a browse yourself a useful tool is located here: http://www.selfseo.com/domain_typo_generator.php

Once you have your list of available misspelled names all you have to do register them with your favorite hosting company and sign up to some affiliate programs.

If the domain you are targeting has an affiliate program itself then sign up for it and use that as your name redirect. That way the user still gets to the exact site they were wanting and you get credited with the commission.

This is a handy little method and can bring in some big cash if you have a lot of domains set up. It can take a little research but like I said I recommend you outsource this to save time. The best thing is once you have set it up you can literally forget about it as it works on autopilot.

When you hit the point where you don't have any left to talk about it's time to search the net for some more content.

There are heaps of article directories outthere with the most well known one being EzineArticles.com.

Simple collect a bunch of articles read them and "re-write" them in your own words. When I say re-write I mean use the software to write the article for you while you speak it. It only takes a couple of hours before you have created 40-50 articles. Then just make sure you go over them and correct any mistakes and theyare ready to be submitted.

There are two main sites that work best for this method. They are www.associatedcontent.com and www.triond.com

You want to sign up to both of these sites and verify your account. Then it's just a matter of submitting articles on a regular basis.

Now this overall method is pretty simple so you can outsource someone to actually use the software and create the articles for you while you just sit back and collect the rewards. Although this is a very simple method it works, it will put cash in your pocket for very little time spent. Try it out see if you can make some money from it and then scale up and increase your profits.

Check out the resources below that you need for this method.

CHAPTER 6

METHOD 4

This method is the classic "Adsense Arbitrage" where you send PPC (pay per click)traffic to your website that has Adsense ads displaying and your Adsense ads make you more money than you are spending on PPC traffic.

Now Google don't particularly like you doing this which is why they bannedpeople from doing this with Adwords.

However you can still do this using the many other PPC networks out there. Thekey is to not make it blatantly obviously that all you are doing is making money from Adsense. The best way to do it is promote an affiliate product as well as have the Adsense ads.

That way you are making an affiliate income plus your Adsense income.

It's very import to track your results here so that you know if you are makingmoney or not.

There is a simple equation you can use to work out what your MINIMUM CTR hasto be for you to break even.

(Adsense Commission x CTR x Clicks) - (Cost per click x clicks) = profit

The Adsense commission is how much Adsense will pay you for every visitor thatclicks on one of your ads. This often varys so it is important to monitor it closely.

The CTR stand for Click Through Rate which means out of all the people who visitor your site how many actually click on your Adsense ads. For example if yousend 1000 visitors to your website and of those 1000 visitors 300 click on your adsense ads you have a CTR of 30%.

The clicks is the total number of people who visited your website. So in the aboveexample the clicks would be 1000.

The other bracket refers to the cost of the PPC traffic. Each PPC network is different and has their own minimum so be sure to calculate this equation for each network you use. I will talk about PPC networks in a moment. But you can get traffic for relatively cheap. So for this example let's say it costs us .05c per visitor and we buy 1000 visitors. So our total cost for this campaign is $50.

Using the equation above you would plug in your Adsense commission, lets say that you make $2 for every person who clicks on your ads. So to find our minimum break even CTR we would have to do the following.

($2 x CTR x 1000) – (.05 x 1000) = $0 which can be broken down to ($2000 x CTR) - ($50) = $0 from here we simply flip it around to equal CTR = $50/$2000 which equals 2.5%

So that means that when we purchase 1000 visitors for $50 we need 2.5% or 250 of them to click on our Adsense ads to break even and not lose any money.

Don't let the maths scare you or confuse you, it's a simple plug in formula to work out what kind of conversion rate we need to NOT lose money.

So in the earlier example above where we said we had 300 people click on our ads from the 1000 we would have a conversion rate of 3% so we would of made a profit with that campaign.

Ok so that's all well and good but what type of stuff can you promote and how do you promote it?

Well I believe the Internet Marketing niche is the best to promote as the keywords usually pay out fairly high on Adsense and it is easy to set up a webpage for it.

You can do this two ways, either set up a simple page on your website or you canuse a free blog such as wordpress.com or blogger.com.

I am not going to go into detail here about setting up a blog or webpage but thereis a heap of free tutorials on the subject and it is a very simple task.

So what we want to do is fill our blog or webpage with relevant unique content.Articles are the best way to go here, you don't have to write a heap of articles your page just needs some unique content.

I recommend that you provide some good useful info for free without any affiliate links at all and then create another article or section on your page promoting a certain product. To find products to promote head over to clickbank.com.

Now what you are going to do is create a webpage or blog that has some useful and helpful unique content and have Adsense ads blend into it. So if you haven't already head over to Adsense.com and set up an account. I'm not going to go into detail about how to place ads etc. as it's clearly explained on the Adsense website.

I also recommend that you promote an affiliate product as well. This acts as a backup plan. Let's say you don't quiet reach the minimum CTR of 2.5% from a campaign you run but you get two affiliate sales worth $47 each you still make a profit from that original ad campaign.

Now time to visit the PPC networks. Adwords is the big dog but there are many many other PPC networks out there that are trying to compete and to do so they offer cheaper prices. This is where we cash in.

I highly recommend you check out the link below. That is a link to the top 10 PPC networks, obviously Google is on top but check out the rest of the list.

But don't just stop at the top ten list. Search the entire site because there are lots of other PPC networks that are constantly running specials and deals you can capitalize on.

This site is a really great site because they review each network and give them a rating. It takes all the guess work out of it.

http://www.payperclicksearchengines.com/directory/top-10-ppc-search-engines/

So in summary you need to:

Set up a blog or website containing new, fresh content in the Internet Marketing niche. Also promote and IM related product to add affiliate income.

Work out your minimum CTR using the equation provided
Create campaigns with some of the other cheap PPC networks
Cash in on adsense and affiliate income ☐

Now it is important to note that you do have to track your results closely and you may have to do some testing and tweaking before you get it right. If you don't getit first go don't be discouraged, keep at it because this does work and once you have it working you can set it on autopilot and have a full time passive income.

CHAPTER 7

METHOD 5

I have recently moved to a large city which has opened my eyes to the power of offline marketing. I got this idea from actually seeing it in action down the street.

It was a simple poster advertising a local dating website. Now I must admit when I first saw it I thought it was stupid and no one would actually bother to write down the URL and visit it but curiosity overpowered me and I visited the site.

Now the site was just a simple redirect to AdultFriendFinder.com which is pretty much the largest dating site out there but he was using his affiliate link. I found it very clever. The key was the domain name was very specific to the area. It pushed the locals angle and it made you think this site was specifically for locals.

So then I started paying more attention and I see these signs everywhere now. Not just that particular one but lots of them.

So I decided to give it a go myself. All you need to do is register a domain name that is local and dating specific. For example: NYSingles.com, Sydneysingles.localdating.com etc.

Be creative but make sure you include the city name and obviously something that lets people know it's a dating site.

Then you will need to create a poster, it can just be a simple A4 size or even smaller it doesn't need to be really big just as long as the URL is clearly displayed. You can do this yourself if you know how or just get it outsourced.

Then go down to your local copy shop and get a whole bunch printed off. They are not very expensive and you will make you money back and then some.

I have found the best places to put these things are obviously the busiest places so big shopping complexes and malls etc.

Public places like that you can just stick them up on sign posts etc.

When you start taking notice you will see them plastered all over the place.

You basically just want to hit the busiest parts of the city, busy intersections and walkways etc.

Put your poster up and watch how much traffic you get. Obviously the more posters you put up the more traffic you will get but it's actually pretty targeted traffic because people actually have to make the effort to either remember your URL or write it down so there is a fair chance they will sign up when they actually visit the site.

Now if you want to take this to the next level you can try and get your poster displayed in pubs and bars. This is a big winner because the majority of people who visit dating sites are male in the first place and nothing beats drunk lonely men who sit at the bar all day trying to find a girl.

So if they see your sign they might say what the hell I'll give it a try.

It can be sometimes difficult to get the owner to agree to put your poster up but then again I guess it depends on where you live and what pubs you go to.

Nightclubs are the real goldmine. Guys pack nights clubs in the hope of getting some action and unfortunately for them the majority go home empty handed and since we live in the technology era most guys are open to hitting the net to see if they have any luck.

So a local ad promoting local singles in a nightclub will definitely get some traffic and if they decide to visit the site when they get home that night I have discovered that drunkenness seems to increase conversion rates.

Another twist to this method is simply advertising in the local personals section of the newspaper. It is a bit more expensive but will most likely have a wider reach.

Depends on the size of your city and the newspaper but if you don't want to physically put up posters everywhere then advertising in the newspaper might be the way to go. Of you could do both!

This is not your traditional type of marketing but it is very effective. Offline marketing is powerful and you can easily take advantage of it if you know how.

CONCLUSION

I hope you have enjoyed this guide. It is filled with different methods that are very creative and some a bit left field. But the most important thing is they bring in the money.

Don't limit your thinking on the amount of ways you can make money online. There are hundreds if not thousands of different methods and tricks and techniques you can do to make money from the Internet.

The ones I have shared with you today are different from the types of things you are probably used to hearing about so I hope that it has opened your eyes to just how much opportunity there is out there and hopefully I have you thinking and you can come up with even more creative ways to make money.

As I have said throughout this guide outsourcing is key here. You can outsource just about all of the methods mentioned in this guide and can you imagine the amount of money you would be bringing in if you had each one of these methods working at its full potential for you every single day.

I have given you what you need, this stuff works, it's proven and tested so go out and make it work for you!

Printed by BoD"in Norderstedt, Germany